My Favorite Dogs

GOLDEN RETRIEVER

Jinny Johnson

A+
Smart Apple Media

Published by Smart Apple Media
P.O. Box 1329
Mankato, MN 56002

Printed in the United States of America,
at Corporate Graphics in North Mankato, Minnesota.

Designed by Hel James
Edited by Mary-Jane Wilkins

Library of Congress Cataloging-in-Publication Data

Johnson, Jinny, 1949-
Golden retriever / by Jinny Johnson.
p. cm. -- (My favorite dogs)
Includes index.
ISBN 978-1-59920-843-5 (hardcover, library bound)
1. Golden retriever--Juvenile literature. I. Title.
SF429.G63J637 2013
636.752'7--dc23
2012008597

Photo acknowledgements
t = top, b = bottom
page 1 iStockphoto/Thinkstock; 3 Jagodka/Shutterstock; 5 Joop Snijder jr./
Shutterstock; 6 iStockphoto/Thinkstock; 7 Hemera/Thinkstock; 8-9 Lisa A.
Svara/Shutterstock; 10-11 iStockphoto/Thinkstock; 12 Comstock/Thinkstock;
13t iStockphoto/Thinkstock, b Mat Hayward/Shutterstock; 14 amidala76/
Shutterstock; 15 Bernd Obermann/Corbis; 16 Apple Tree House/Thinkstock;
17 Tom Nebbia/Corbis; 18-19 Ryan McVay/Thinkstock; 20 iStockphoto/
Thinkstock; 21 Michelle D. Milliman/Shutterstock; 23 tstockphoto/Shutterstock
Cover Onur ERSIN/Shutterstock

DAD0504
042012
9 8 7 6 5 4 3 2 1

Contents

I'm a Golden Retriever!

I'm a friendly, happy dog
and I'm loyal to my owners.

I love to please people
so I'm very obedient,
but I like to play as well.

What I Need

I'm quite big and I like plenty of exercise. I love to swim, too. I like being part of the family and I'm not a good guard dog because I'm so friendly!

Best of all, I love to bring back sticks and balls if you throw them for me.

The Golden Retriever

Double-layer coat; outer layer straight or wavy

Strong tail

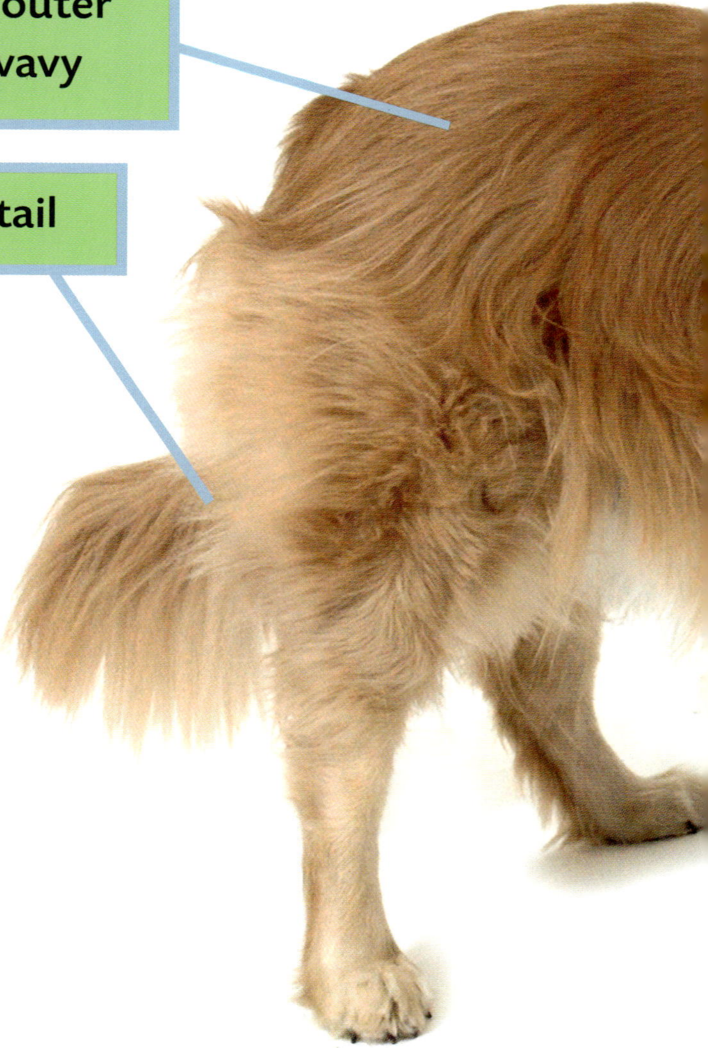

Color:
cream to golden

Weight:
55–75 pounds
(25–34 kg)

Height:
up to 24 inches
(61 cm)

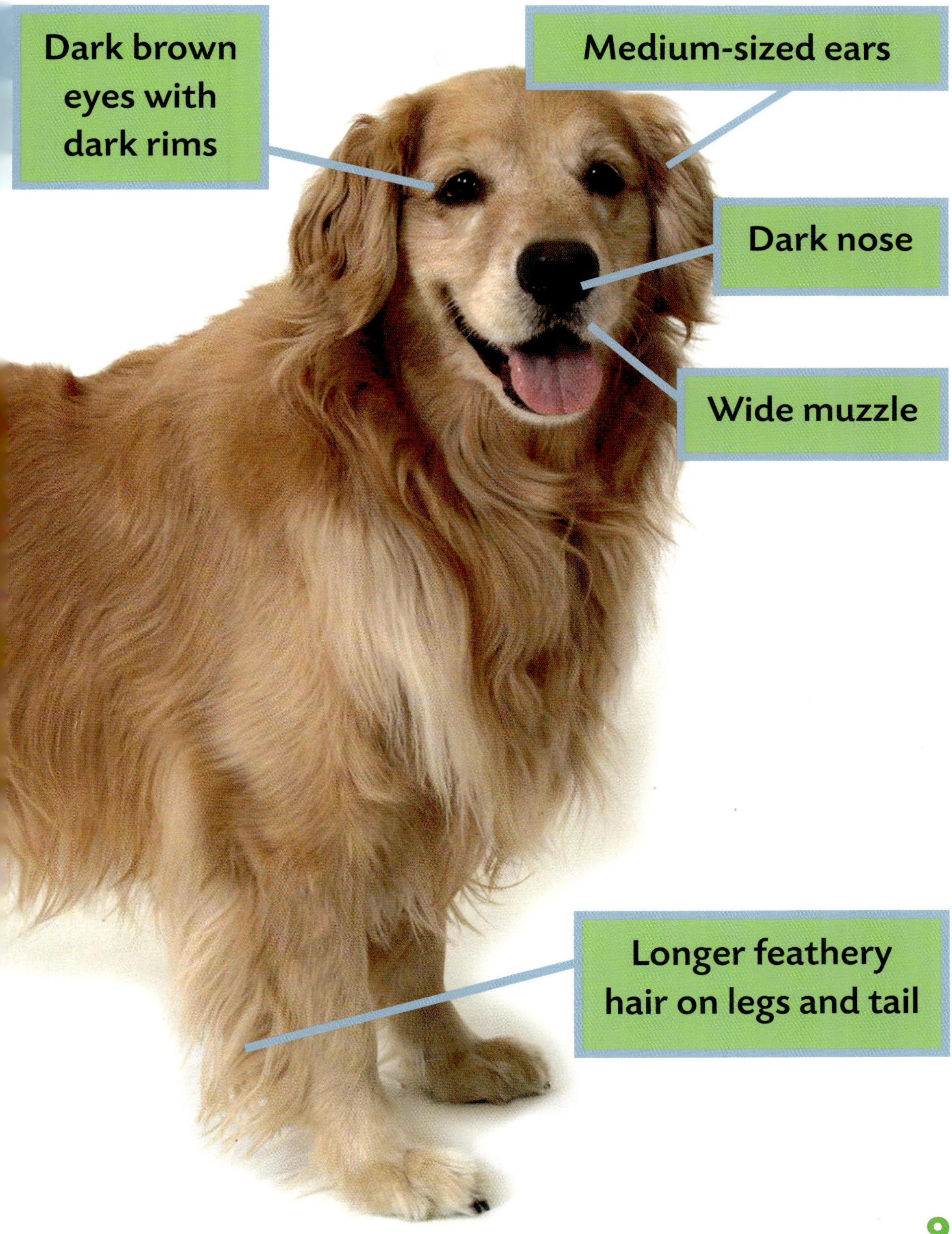
Dark brown eyes with dark rims
Medium-sized ears
Dark nose
Wide muzzle
Longer feathery hair on legs and tail

All About Golden Retrievers

This dog was first bred in Scotland to fetch (retrieve) birds, such as ducks, shot by hunters.

Don't worry, this is a pretend duck. The dog is being trained to bring things back to its owner.

A golden retriever can hold objects very carefully in its mouth and bring them back to its owner.

Growing Up

Golden retriever puppies need to be with their mom until they are about eight weeks old. When you take your puppy home, she may be frightened at first.

She will miss her family, so be very kind and gentle while she gets used to you.

Working Dogs

Golden retrievers are intelligent dogs. They are quick learners and like to obey their owners, so they are easy to train.

This dog is helping to find a missing person.

Some work as search and rescue dogs. They help firemen and policemen find injured people after accidents.

Helping People

Golden retrievers are also trained as service dogs to help people with disabilities. They can learn to switch on lights, open doors, and even help people to get dressed.

A golden retriever starred in the film *Homeward Bound: The Incredible Journey.*

Water Dogs

Golden retrievers are good swimmers and take any chance for a dip. They love to fetch sticks thrown into the water.

Never let your dog go for a swim on her own. She could run into trouble.

Your Healthy Golden Retriever

These dogs can have hip problems, so you need to have a puppy checked before buying.

Your golden retriever will need brushing at least once a week to get rid of any loose hair. Check for fleas, too.

In summer, your dog may shed more hair and need brushing daily.

Golden retrievers will swim anywhere. Your dog might need a bath after a dip in a muddy pond.

Caring for Your Golden Retriever

You and your family must think carefully before buying a golden retriever. She will live for at least ten years and need lots of attention.

Every day your dog will need food, water, and exercise, as well as lots of love and care. You will also need to take her to the vet for regular checks and vaccinations. When you and your family go out or away on vacation, you will have to make plans for your dog to be looked after.

There has been a golden retriever in the White House. President Gerald Ford owned a golden retriever named Liberty.

Useful Words

muzzle
The long face of an animal such as a dog.

retrieve
To bring something back.

vaccination
An injection that protects your dog from certain illnesses.

Index